There Is Blue Somewhere

Cyberwit.net
HIG 45 Kaushambi Kunj, Kalindipuram
Allahabad - 211011 (U.P.) India
www.cyberwit.net
Tel: +(91) 9415091004 +(91) (532) 2552257
E-mail: info@cyberwit.net

Lay-out inside: monoeil.be
Printed at Repro India Limited.

To Rozalina, Eva, Nikola and Kalina

There Is Blue Somewhere

Alternative Reading ScenarioıɹɐuǝɔS ɓuıpɐǝᴚ ǝʌıʇɐuɹǝʇl∀

- Book of Life
- Currents
- Mare Nostrum
- Of Ancient Books and Maps, the Quest and the Sea
- In Honor of Hugo Pratt
- The Day After
- Pictures of an Exhibition at Chhatrapati Shivaji Maharaja Vastu Sangrahalaya (Formerly Prince of Wales Museum of Western India), Mumbai
- There Can Only Be One
- Modest & Free Interpretation of a Mussorgsky: VIII.
- Boy in a Box
- We Dance to It
- Ominous They Stand
- Red River
- No Nightingales in Nicosia
- Barcelona: IV
- Maze Inc.
- Barcelona: I
- Hunting Season
- I Am the Last Poet
- The Habit of Speaking
- Modest & Free Interpretation of a Mussorgsky: II.
- It's Not the Stars Which Are Important
- Magic Dreams
- What Is Life?
- Cardinal Points

Book of Life

when I turn the pages
of deep blue seas
I wave my sails
peacefully quilted
with parts of tales
never told.

yellow yearns the sun
attempting
to stay afloat.

Cycle of Eternity

Currents

the world is suffering from bulimia
magical realism
of packed warehouses
sniffed milk powder bags
a pardon of udders once milked
hormonal forgiveness full of steroid antibiotics

the world is suffering from anorexia
expressionism
of overflying cargo planes
treeless mountains bombarded with flower
of departing troops and abandoned refugees
left to the enemy's free hand

the world is suffering from neurosis
abstract conceptualism
of ecological certification
of polished projectiles
of unique idemtity
brand-conscious branding
of consumption of child labor
and dissociating ethically

the world is suffering from psychosis
surrealism
of applying double standards
of peace be with you
whilst piercing the heart
and gagging the mouth
of sex slaves, child soldiers, disaster sales and statistics viewing

the world suffers from
forgive us because
we didn't plan(t) it this way

Mare Nostrum

I present you on a tray
- the head of Jochanaan -
look into the lens, mirror of the soul

I twitter my lesser thoughts
- stream of conscience -
facts, figures, graphs to left-swipe
in a thumbs-up trance
my status is my creed

I walk on water
- I could sail or split it -
the buoyancy of toddlers
as sirens guard the graveyards

I fill the moon with the blood of the damned
- reflection in the salted sea -
the call of carcasses in cooling vans stranded alongside the yellow big road
pickled dreams

I write what not wants to be read
- building blocks of Babel -
Cries of impotence, studies filled with numbers, reports with values
scanning destruction

I gave you fire to burn away the image,
water to deepen the distance

Sid Meier's War on Terror

Hold your spine
Straighten your shout
Iron your posture
Stand together
Be as one

Topsy turvy swipes the enemy two hexagons further

Heyhey sighs the fresh farmer, created to be working on the land
at the border
bringing food to the silos, to the soldiers.
Feed to fall on fields of honor

choose your armor
women descending stairs
men staring testosterone

They won't come in pieces, but as our biggest fear
Take part in the revolution! It will be televised!

Drop those bombs
Gas these minorities
Collect points, deduct donations

All in your strife for innocence

Take the eye of the other to read a book
Show the other cheek, don't question authorities
Press enter, shut down, re-start
Do not install Paradise.

Drone Talk Transcripts #1: The Official Version

[snake72]   We are now tracking three vehicles going south

[orchid54]   Roger, ground force commander's intent is to destroy the vehicles and the personnel, right now lotus87 is showing that the individuals aggressing the vehicles are holding cylindrical objects in their hands »radio static«

static radio shatter

[snake72]   Roger, go back there, do you see a riffle

[orchid54]   affirmative, that IS a riffle

[snake72]   Roger orchid54, please advise, it is a riffle

[orchid54]   Roger that, you have the authority to wipe them bastards out

[snake72]   Roger orchid54, will do so with pleasure, lock on missile

static radio shatter

[lotus87]   radio static is served!

static radio shatter

[lotus87]   don't let it go cold! »radio static« I'll bin it. You won't »radio static« food

[snake72]   »radio static« mission completed, goin' back to base.

The Holy Trinity Bus Poem

be on time!
see the heritage
check in, passport, ticket ready,
be on time!
Motherfucker, shit, shit!

tell a story
emotion and spine
capture the thread
a life, all mine
me, the Motherfucker, shit, shit!

nothing happened
God will punish in the end
Motherfucker, shit, shit!

orphaned by hateful eyes
in his brain the thought he had
completely untrue, totally sad
Motherfucker, shit, shit!

whitewashed memories
drowned in wine
words are the poison of the brain
Motherfucker, shit, shit!

thunder was never that close
burn blue in screens
submerged in tweets and likes
unfollow posts you do not like
unlike friends you never see
untangle threads of you and me
Motherfucker, shit, shit!

no alternative to your facts exists
no solution found
to the acid in your words
hit the road
parents make up for the wrong done to you
Motherfucker, shit, shit!

stories need to be retold
listen up 140-character people
this is not forgotten
Motherfucker, shit, shit!

Conventional Stereotypes

O thank you, sir
are you sure?
white people sit always in the back sir
they are afraid of us 'Brownies' - I refrained from pointing out that a
brownie was a chocolate-based cake - and took my normal place
I felt good, in control, although the driver was sitting next to me
much more relaxed than Mumbai
here we are calmer sir, no poverty but prosperity
no beggars but shopping malls
a night train rushes overhead
from the north sir, that train took four days to get here sir, from here you
can go all up sir, all the way to the mountains.
as the roads get smaller and the headlights scarcer, I contemplate the more
than one thousand six hundred kilometers of
highway in full renovation.

9/11 Memorial / One WTC

so, there you are
Your existence is real
carved in stone
nor name nor body
but yet so alive
in the eyes of so many
passers-by ɘiⱦlɘƨ-ing themselves with you
at yet another
landmark
in yet another
city
on yet another
continent
but You, You will not see
L'Origine du monde
no strolls along the Hudson
no cruise on the Nile
no bathing in the Ganges
no *Schönen Blauen Donau*
no voyage to *The Heart of Darkness*

water of life
falls down
perpetual motion
bringer of life
an inundation of tears
make emotions freeze
clean shaven cheeks
turn red

memories of my twins -
they do not understand -
others just watch, point, picture
click-shutter-click
blink of an eye
capture the void
wait in line to see more memorial

the horseman behind a double fence
praising freedom and revenge
a body for an eye
click-shutter-click
the blink of an eye
all is gone
a final blow
cloud of dust

the wind strikes me
ice cold
reality cripples my bones
the Hudson flows before my eyes
joggers with apps
dog show dog owners
encounter TV-staring strangers
another ɘiɬlɘꙅ
click-shutter-click
blink of an eye
all eyes on dog
woof   good girl   sit   bye
the dog wants to move on
wants to pee
mark territory - I was here -
so other dogs know
she was there.

would You have liked dogs?
Playdoh, dolls or cars
Mickey or Spiderman?
would you have wanted to become
ballet dancer or fire fighter?
or would you have preferred to write
on a bench
on the banks of the Hudson
in the freezing cold?

as I feel the kicks of my unborn child
I tell tales to a tummy
of water
bringing life

—

This poem was dedicated to Dianne T. Singer and Jennifer L. Howley and their unborn children.
Written on a bench on the banks of the Hudson River, New York, USA on November 16, 2014.

Molenbeek

a heron gazes a murky brook
no tick, no blink, no shudder
waiting for the right prey to pass through the visor
four male drakes play in nearby puddles

chasing possible partners
a pair of coots paddle past
bickering with some gulls roaming the banks
between the reed autumn mosquitos mix with ladybugs and ephemera
into a smooth buzzing mist.

—

Written on a bench on the banks of the brook Molenbeek, November 19th, 2015 at the Boudewijn Parc, Jette (Brussels Capital Region, Belgium).

Path of Dreams

In Honor of Hugo Pratt

A black line
seagulls pass
sails set to move away
a silent breeze caresses
the marram bows
dunes nor waves

Meanwhile.....

Pictures of an Exhibition at Chhatrapati Shivaji Maharaja Vastu Sangrahalaya (Formerly Prince of Wales Museum of Western India), Mumbai

look at Arachnida, weaving divine intervention
her fingers seem invisible
an inspiration for the thousands underaged cramped in backstreet boxes
creating the finest cloth
fashionista worthy

Cloth is our second skin.
our first home out of the womb

the little girl on the street awaits reincarnation
as she begs to feed her offspring
look and behold:
'a difference in the indifference of passers-by'

the shining golden Sunday bests of the local women
contrasts heavily against the baggy anonymity of westerners
a blonde exception wearing sports shorts is a recurrent ɘɿɒʌz
accompaniment
her smile and pose cosmetic
her boyfriend jealously proud
they follow the path instructed by the 'free for foreigners' audio guided
tour'

the deconstruction of the clothing worn is a fine thread, running through
the littlest's fingers - manual labor saves energy and is so much more
eco-friendly - into the mother's loom. Generations of experience provide
efficiency and quality.

Thread is a pathway a line to follow
through the passage of life

where will the little girl sleep tonight?
will she sing lullabies to her two children?
she has a king's wish - as they say - a boy and a girl
trained in the art of begging
his proficiency level is already high
'Wealth sets you free' a billboard states at the slums
soon he'll leave the sweet smelling of fermented shrimps and excremental
waste

this Tinseltown make-believe
soothes my mind
what beast am I to discard reality?
an inner cry for justice
as the beasts of previous incarnations
eat me from the inside
my stomach goes through a carrousel of
resentment, hate, anger, loathing, bereavement, acceptance, fear and
compassion
the spices of life define our species

All religions are branches of one tree - the Tree of Life (1)

in a murky covered corridor,
mustached men sell electric torches and dildos
similar sized objects in silver, ivory or baby pink
further on, a disabled man glues soles into shoes
chatting to his neighbor in front
repairing a broken-down smartphone
at the end 'sir, here sir' sit two boys
in pole position to shine shoes
in front of them the remnants
of what has been a man, sleeping – I guess –
worse off than that guy I passed earlier - near the sari and jeans stalls -
who could hide underneath a black umbrella, that one could impose some
privacy towards the passing crowds.

incense burns my nostrils hiding the other odeurs of human excrements
white shirts reflect the midday sunlight
crisp and crease folded perfectly
warmth weighs upon my lungs

as I cough out metro-building-site-dust and diesel fumes
'progress is coming' a metro announcement billboard predicts
it'll guide tourists more directly towards the key touristic sites
luckily, I skipped the bold idea to visit the meat markets
I reach my trusted water seller
he doesn't remember me
too busy to process this cane into sap
I like his stall because of his enchanted sound extracting contraption
a mantra of singing wheels, clanging chains and train like noises
escape the hand-turned machinery

he reaches out to the warm water bottles
ignoring his ice turning into water fridge-like structure
so, he does remember me - I try to see a glimpse of recognition but fail -
which is better than being chatted-up to buy
even the broadest smile is to be rewarded
the musical mantra restarts

Epilogue:
Looking through the airplane window I see a deep orange and Munch-red
sky (is this an Air India wink? No! Even the polished stewardess gazes
out of the window in awe) over a thick tea-with-milk brown blanket of
clouds. Is this blood flowing across the horizon from a divine struggle?
And if so, who won?
Or lies that answer in the sunrise, in tons of food waste being dumped,
or in the cloth, the cover of a crying baby, shivering in an air-conditioned
world?

Meaning

for thoughts to be possible, the meaning is the impossible
think about meaning
be mean about thinking
ting ting
for whom the bell tolls
balls toll around in the universe
but the universe, life, anything, only has value through thought.
no value through markets no market shares no shares no sharing just
caring

Free thinking is giving no value to things, ideas, feelings ...
Free thinking is without value
Free thinking is impossible to value
Free thinking is impossible
Free thinking is valuing the impossible
Free thinking is a feeling
Free thinking is an idea

Free thinking is a business
Free thinking is valuing the possible
Free thinking is possible
Free thinking is a feeling
Free thinking is an idea
Free thinking is thinking.
Free thinking is freedom
Free thinking is giving no value to things, ideas, feelings

Hunting Season

There should be a hunting season for karaoke singers
'To be shot
between 10pm and midnight'

In a parallel world
oversized butterflies
have tattoos of binge drinking Brits on their buts

On the road to Oz
toads were more attracted to storks
flies to frogs
than foam to the beer in the bar downstairs

But the beer was not what bothered
the haunted squealing
- the end of the world? -
as the volcano contemplated erupting

But that would be too much fame
for The Wigan Arms
as the Moon, Venus and Mars danced to the tunes the drunk
burped into the cloudless night-time skies.

Magritte Tie with Eyes

I dare to stare at the tie

———————————— B R E A K ————————————

eyes dare to stare at the tie

———————————— B R E A K ————————————

the tie is knotted under a watchful eye

watch the paper plain
watch eyes tie the knot
watch the time
watch the tie
watch white collar with tie
watch blue collar
 the sky
watch white cloud be collared
watch the eye
on me
watch me
with tie
eye in the sky
fly by
collar bye

I watch the eye flying by
I try not to cry
just pry or spy
the passersby my tie
prying and spying
as I try
to fit in
fitting
the suit, the tie o why

A well-tied tie is the first serious step in life.

don't ever let love and loyalty leave you.

tie them around your neck and write them on your heart.

be.smart
the art
of tying the knot
coloring the sky
to live by
to vouch
to not untie
the daring staring eye
It always sees you
the eye

———————————— B R E A K ————————————

———————————— B R E A K ————————————

Full stop

The Habit of Speaking

<Paroles et paroles et paroles>

the habit of speaking about the immediate needs of life, requires words
which designate a limited sense to the objects but also to itself.

talk about one's self, the meaning of self, of me, of I
three ways of looking at myself
through the looking glass
through the mirror
through the ɘɼ̃ʃɘƨ
through the meaning of I
looking through the eye
looking through the self
shelves of meaning
branded by others than the self
branded by others to give meaning to the self
branded so others create meaning for themselves

an object does not tent to its name that much that it cannot find itself a
more suitable one.

pick a name
pick an object
let the object pick its own name

no names left unturned
no object unnamed
no name
just a number
a barcode

swipe left right up down

update new programs

bug fixes

new features

more features

faster
faster
more
more
faster

bug
fixes
bug
fixes
bug
fix
F-Ix
X
X
= the Unknown
equation
equal

all bugs are equal
some bugs are more equal than others

the others

defined by the self
defined by the mirror
defined by the looking glass
defended by none
nonexistent

but because of the self
because of me
because of I
eye with which we see
do we see
what we see what we mean

is seeing believing?
do you believe
the blue sky
the cloud
the all-seeing eye

I
Me
Myself

you see?

Monument Valley: Ocher Maze

Ominous they Stand

ominous they stand
waiting to get woken
their tasks at hand
all lined up in clusters
guarding the murky waters
as oil painted swabs of red-white, blue-white dissolving into the bottom
brownness
who said seas were blue?
earthy colors reclaimed them
is this a graveyard of used industry?
a reminder of the stages of progress
bouncing on the water
between the buoyancy of diesel and debris
we proceed to carve the littered sea
on the rhythm of an old engine and worn out planks asphalted together
on rusty vats a single seagull sits and stares
contemplating the thick humid sky
resting like a warm winter quilt onto the water
somewhere above there is a blue sky
existing in memories and oral history
messages in a bottle

Paradise by the Lakeside

this is paradise
although mosquitoes tend to
seek food for their offspring
only distant coconut cutting
Krishna chanting
make one suspect
a human presence
as birds mark their territory
a plastic bottle floats past
message of precarious hubris
a faraway thunder roars
as if to underline that point
monsoons are not over sir
rain brings life
a tsunami came ashore
many souls serve another body now
it's religion which is killing us sir
and borders
do flies stop at the border?
fish follow the currents
only in the forest now, there are snakes
they used to be everywhere
and they were respected
the road to paradise was air conditioned
full of holes
and educational
dogs compete with monkeys
but that's at the other side of the river
here birds and butterflies share the space
I never felt lonely here
but very much alone
longing for home
travel always seems
romantic at the offset
these words are guardsmen of the experience
a sole frog agrees

Mountain of Fat

the Mountain of Fat was diluted into the Southern Backwaters
on Monroe Island
a prawn patch seems filled with carcasses
a hawk screeches just before the thunderstorm
nature is getting greener
ready to accept the rain in her already flooded womb
I meet the mooing
grazing on the banks
providing the soundtrack of this journey

we're covering the world with cellulose
hoping to preserve it
though our sell-by-date is near

five minutes, he said an hour ago,
the slight summer rain became a drench
Thor was really fighting hard
but he was fighting on foreign soil
a third eye was looming on the other side of the vastness of water
getting filled
there is blue somewhere
between the earthy ochers and greens

It's not the Stars Which are Important

it's not the stars which are important
it's the darkness in our eyesight
what is the surrounding in which you thrive?
inside the bubble gum bubble
I hear people chatting in the darkness
sharing their secrets under a mosquito net
the mating of the crickets disturbs evening prayer chants
a late train hoots past on a distant track
people will reach their destination
in time this all will disappear
there is no goal to be reached
life itself is a challenge
not to be taken lightly
no stars tonight
just the sizzling of spices
and the humming of mosquitos
hovering nearby
life treats them well
there are even rains
after the monsoon has gone
offspring is rich
diner is plentiful
or brings the night breakfast
and wishes for long life?

What Defines Us is How we Rise After we Have Fallen

what philosophy shares with poetry is that there are no answers
which doesn't mean there shouldn't be questions asked

mosquitoes are eager to visit the library

poetry is like an ocher beach
wondering why the ocean has left

but luckily, there is the sea, I mesmerized, during the lecture of the teacher
to the village women.

standing around the microphone is a crowd trying to make out
who's saying what, when. the village people are in awe of so many
organizational talents working together for the bettering of their lives.
they want to suck out the last words out of the communion of poets
gathered to enlighten themselves with words of wisdom. the sun finds
a way to boil the water in our bodies, but the sea is close by, so that's a
comforting thought.

the sea should just be sea
the waves may not be confined to
concrete jaws

you build a big wall and your soul is confined within the wall, the teacher
tells the gazing crowd. they are in awe with his politically
correct interpretations of the works of the poets who have
appeared in front of them.
the Chinese daughter dances over the wall, confining the shrine within its
garden, she applauded the public before gracefully jumping to another
part of the wall. her soul seems very free, on top of that wall, close by the
sea.

the crows are back, screeching their agreement to the shouting teacher, he
confines the rainbow in the text to a unicolored shade of red ocher beach
sand.

Ma'at

I arrive at the end of this level
the crows accompanied me to the steps of this next incarnation

all hail to the teachings of the poets
enlightenment is near

we thank the people thanking people who are thanking people who
thanked those present who did thank the people earlier

at the beach a bra washed ashore
sparkling a glimpse of imagination.

Past the Darkest Hour

past the darkest hour
the axe turns into a new dawn
I gaze at the maze beneath me
stretched cloth of threads, gold, silver
sparkling glitter
two dimensions become three
geometric welcome into a New World
a cheering child welcomes touchdown

all of you returned to your daily routine
I miss my tree, the lamp post
the brook shimmering in the shining sun

the Minotaur descended into its new labyrinth
next level in the game
a quest for a souvenir, two birthday presents, a Refugio Nomada, a poet,
an interesting intervention, a temple, Frida's place, my Spanish language
memory and the way back to my Ariadne.

Maze Inc.

friendly but correct
caring and altruistic
I was stamped, an entrance to the maze,
at first seemingly daunting
seems seamless and smiling
first hurdle taken
follow the threaded labyrinth
relax and release extra weight
contribute to the local waste problem

il est trois heures
l'aéroport se réveille

palm trees wave in the lukewarm sky
the scent of tarmac and diesel
the rustle of a concrete boarded highway
pitching higher as the fence encases a yet empty metro station

white lights color green in tunnels
luckily, I have offline maps
so, the taxi driver monocles where his sedan will take him
flyovers and arriving in middle of a sleeping suburb
a door without a doorbell
a whisper of the taxi driver I need to keep a low profile here

crickets sing
under rows upon rows
yellow and green party flags
a perpetual fiesta
are they the hired mariachi band?
A sealed metal door
recently - not so recently - painted
white

a few doors further
a muffled telephone conversation
joins in the soundscape

the crickets become basso continuo
layered by distant cars
a short typical latin american piston sound of a bus
a motorcycle
a whirring truck
complete the lower parts of the music bar

the light inside - I spy underneath a crack between the rusty door and
polished smog-blackened concrete slabs - is of a blueish white quality
artificial shades paint
other concrete slabs
needlessly squared in a row
pedestrian heaven

there is no rock to put a key underneath
this is not the road to Bethlehem but Eucalipto

contemplating if the added sounds
on the highway getting busier
gave me their blessings to wake up those behind the locked compound
even if it was ok, they are non-reachable
sleep has covered them, paralyzed their communication equipment

I minimize myself
blend in with the alcove
surrounding the much anticipated - but not opening - white metal door

the police patrol the streets
blue-red-white are their lights
they slow down and inspect
me waiting

staring at the white door

reaching out for those inside

no roaming is
no connection to virtuality
real cats gaze at me, intruder into their realm

inside my bag they scent a goal
they are shyer than the Sofia Gurkostreet pack of dogs
but they are imminently present
they startle at a faraway telephone ringing
gazing at me with a weary smile
caught on their roaming path
a neighbor walks his dog
cat gone

all silent but the crickets
the whirring trucks

we all know
we are all here
we all have our position
we all wait and watch
white f

Magic Dreams

Magic Dreams
'Se renta'
cannabis and excrements
Bellas Artes Santa Veracruz
concentrated urine
a public toilet
familiar glocalised smells
order is more enforced
when tourist droves arrive
the friendliness of the uniformed
is touching

Sun Rise
I wash my hands
the Rains the Floods the Music the Heart

I enter the world's navel
humble
I bow to the Tlatoani
rejuvenated at the holy tree
burn the old self
let the snake steal my ashes

coffee with canella and cacao

Barcelona

I

a non-saucy sauce sprinkled
over the absentee baby squids
a conversation about language
as a history of content
the tapas taste tantalizing as the Babylonians converse in terms of world
politics
peas are absent
a loop station of speed dating
matches distant family members
what do a showering cello, a mediaeval square finger drum and amplified
guitar have in common but a tantric bathing in a troubadour language?
every word is a cry for freedom
oppression does not silence the desire
to express the circumventing of a reality
which has been denied a Wilsonian status
a quintet of fears
a nation which is
a map of yellow ribbons
a geopolitical cake crumbles
a nation of nations
a state of statements
a union disbanding itself
wir schaffen es (nicht!)
exile
ex l'ïlle
an island battered by a tempest
no island but attached
glued mountains to *al tierra iberica*
cured and sliced

La Sagrada Familia sheds light
onto pilgrims, tourists, (dis)believers
soldiers seem alien as they wage
a war
as the sun sets
on stage XI

an ascending golden 'imago'
is supported

sanctus sanctus sanctus
sanctus sanctus sanctus sanctus
sanctus sanctus sanctus sanctus sanctus
sanctus sanctus sanctus sanctus sanctus sanctus
sanctus sanctus sanctus sanctus sanctus sanctus sanctus

I can see clearly now
the rain has gone
I can see butt obstacles in my way

II

do I cite
those
who were
whom I've read
whom I admired
whom I admire
whom I will admire
whom I would have admired
if I
I was
when my life was before
in a state of cliterature
trying to pronounce
your essence
in just one
one single
one continuous stroke
of a lingua franca
purely vowels and nasal consonants
I do not yearn
for my extasy
if there is naught
we are two
we are one
we are
we
you
1

III

all members of the audience
straightened their backs
when a 'penis' was shown
in a poem on the stage
a drop of a pin lasted the pin-drop silence
the cello is a wonderful instrument
a reflection made
monotone and monochrome
hermits display their sonority
the content is all
but the marketeer seeks packaging
an angle to have a free entrance into
what must have been an exciting mental
orgasm
as the blue light stares at the rabbits in the open-roofed box
the poetess scrambles her bag
running back
to accept praise
the distance to be covered
is like an ocean without a current
wind still
waiting
waving
on the raft of the Medusa.

IV

churches burn
incense but innocence
purification or iconoclasm
as we all deal with heritage
we speak a common tongue
anarchy of colors
fade to black
violent teddy bears man the barricades
there is no such thing as a free state
noncommittal swirls of cigar smoke
in thin air
a gush of warm current
draws borders
whilst suits and cravats
sip coffee
on a non-existing map
talkative as may be the waving flags
yet balconies are the territorial combat
to which the discourse is withdrawn
Is there a bird - not caged - that longs to praise its liberty?
Is there a mountain - still standing - shedding tears of solitude?
Is there a plain - unfenced - that yearns to be scorched?
Is there a river - yet to trace its source - that gushes wildly?
Is there a sea - yet to beach - that touches the sky?
as we all are guided blindly
into a conflict of interests
a rewriting of a man-made mushroom cloud
fire and fury
bullying the bully
great again
is the grieving
of the archetypal mother
losing her offspring
to a cause
lost

there is a blue sky to be found
over the rainbow
but there will be no tapping of red heels
just

the gushing of blood

                                        clotted onto the pavement
                              where once this child drew
                        a chalked paradise
                  of non-digested tales
            midst the rumbling ruins
of a suppressed storyline
one voice one vote
vetoed
capital
mistake
guillotined
from A to z
            z
            z
            z
            z
            z
            z
            z
            z
            Z
            Z
            Z
            Z
            Z
            Ztsj_{Op}

V

and if I also crave
to discuss the battery time
of my electronic devises
on how one needs to drag
the prolongation of reach-ableness
the updating of the terms and conditions
the thumb tiredness
of too distant or too small
tabs to be closed
as poets recite the cravings of their soul

I follow their index finger
caressing the typos
on the pages of their copy
of a book printed
translates
analyzed
white space
- white noise between
stanzas -
stands sole
waiting for
a squeeze of lime
spicing the page numbers
as the index is missing
the chronological map
a reading direction
unorthodox
rides a dragon
hesitation of dry forms
and formalistic prose
is there a voice
a cry in the dark
a tactile structure
of hand-crafted paper sheeting

cut to size
by the editor
not by the text
the introduction precludes

the applause follows as automated end
the silence
structures the reading
borders the print
underlines the orality
for whom tolls the bell
but for the end
of time

to spice the lamb
to skewer the truth
there is no beginning
there is no end

only the archaeology of transience
of beaches and life vests
of tides
of periods
of eras
of what others will guard
and yet others revive
and yet others study
if any
if any
if any

as our voices fade
the apparatus creaks
falls over
reinvents itself
only the archaeology of transience

of beaches and life vests
of tides
of periods
of eras
if any
if any
if any

I also crave
to discuss the battery time
of my electronic devises
if any
if any
if any
waste

The Bystander Effect

Boy in a Box

rattling toys
eagerness
mama's taco stand
cars wait and enter the public parking
cries of joy

they all pass without

all the gold has gone
it ordains innermost sacred spaces
where worship awaits it
conquistador's voyeurism
displays of suffering
exaltation sadism
as we rule the earth
it was given to us
master of our environment

we act as spoiled children
never satisfied

the torture of greed
the original sin was not
knowledge nor carnal pleasure
but the urge to exploit
the colonization of have-nots
the monopoly of male ignorance
because they cannot grow life
destruction is their concept
a circle of fertility
their goal is to pierce, seed and leave
and not able to copulate
their urge becomes anger
inventing the concept of soul
the sacrifice of blood
to fertilize an uncertain will of
a higher cosmic being

inventing straight lines and archetypes
disguising that women are better equipped
they care for knowledge
they share themselves with the beginning of life

we, the white cis-male, shaped a world to our mirrored image
claiming it, because

I can only apologize
knowing
this will never
ever be enough

May I call you Esperanza?
as I'm just a minotaur on a quest
I beg you
unleash your triple cultural heritage
unbox your life
teach me to explore
beyond what the faults of my ancestry

ustedes son nuestra esperansa real

Red River

there is a river, you know
the water flows
to an ocean
life flows through it

there is a river, you know
trees on the banks
reeds wave on the rhythm
life flows through it

there is a river, you know
tides and rains feed it
watering fertile lands
life flows through it

there is a river, you know
too many times
the river turns red
life flows through it

there is a river, you know
banks, littered
aspirations, hopes, futures
life flows through it

there is a river, you know
a whole generation perished
trying to wade through it
life flows through it

there is a river, you know
life flows through it
the river turned red
the river turned red
life flows through it

there is a river, you know
every country has a river
every country has a generation
coloring rivers red
with their lives
washed away
within the reeds
between the trees
washed up on the other bank

Of Ancient Books and Maps, the Quest and the Sea

we cross the Mediterranean
draw lines on a map
color coastlines, name places markers
describe our Odyssey
in the midst of the sea
in the midst of the water-plain
lies land
feet on firm fertile soil
on our way to
Elsewhere

O Captain! My Captain!
Thou wereth taken in chains
Who speaketh of the suffering and the sea

who teaches us the value of life

behold the sea,
Pathos,
on the other side, there

we read ancient books
verse, meter, heros
survival, alive
every crossing orange vests float
untold tales
- fish feed -
blot into the see

orange bobs   orange bobs   orange bobs   orange bobs   orange bobs
        orange bobs   orange
orange bobs   orange bobs   orange bobs   orange bobs
                          orange bobs
                                            orange bobs

bobs orange bobs orange bobs orange bobs orange
orange bobs orange bobs orange bobs orange bobs
bobs orange bobs Your text here 1 orange bobs orange bob orange

We Dance to it

we closed our eyes
smiles broken; lips sealed - a dream galloping away
what did we do?
But hurry past
remembering how we marked time together
washing our guilt
in the rat race
with lavender and lime
an orphan's cry, music to our ears
what did we do?
But stare into the void
smiles broken; lips sealed - a dream galloping away
we closed our eyes

"Life tests me
it exhausts me
it is a daily struggle
that leaves bruises daily"

who looks and sees?
my daily struggle?
I stare into the void
smile broken, lips sealed - my dream galloping away
remembering how time marked me
I dissolve into
the daily noises
a faint memory of a past happiness
my daily struggle
but who looks or sees?

"Life tests me
it exhausts me
it is a daily struggle
that leaves bruises daily"

the world closes its eyes
smiles broken; lips sealed - a dream galloping away
not even a footnote in the news
the body - a soul
the dream – gallo(ping away)

Take this Body, Break it, and Forget I ever Existed

an object seizes to exist once it has been given a name by men

history should become her story

glocalisation is situating the own ego on a Mercator projection map
knowing it is not the real representation of how the universe perceives the
planet we are depleting towards the next mass extinction of ourselves.

every time we meet each other I wish we became vegetarian

take this body, break it, and forget I ever existed

the sea gave birth to Cyprus

in the middle of the forest a silent song awaits singing

No Nightingales in Nicosia

there we are, the not so anonymous authors taking their stance
in the circle
lavender, royalty, his-story, central eclecticisms
building relations, high society, fairy tale footprints
a room and a view
a dancing dervish taints the wall on the other side
in a no-man's-land a watchtower not watching no man no land
a perfectly circular city scarred by his-story   again

her story rubs salt on her baby
her story seems lost in translation
her story sheds salted tears
faith boxes people
calves to be led
to the altar of slaughter
to be boxed   again

nails hammer
lids close
cheaper options
in human composting
moral compasses turn
go warn the women
"be mourning mothers!"   again

the gates of hell are slowly opened
by the arms of tweeting men
in is poured the ammunition stored
out swarm the mortals in misery
screams on screens are duly documented
sorrows posted on profile pages
empathy is a distance to bridge   again

but there are no nightingales in Nicosia, tonight
except in the karaoke bar
we scream at screens and selfie our stream
we forget, we feast, are a one-minute star
we saw, we gave, we discuss, and we wave
we forget our fears in a mourning jar
sleepwalking in genocide   again

Modest & free Interpretation of a Mussorgsky

I

distance is a particle
time is a wave
words out of proportion
hold the pen
write the letter
wipe the surface
blotted paper
everlasting ink
his thoughts get stuck at the 'p' of 'poet'
carve the 'm' with a needle
flood the cracks with meaning
large rivers separate longing from upstream punctuation
sail around consonants
get trapped by vowels in a puddle.

—

Chinese ochre Rorschach
no dotted cows on the striped wallpaper
he sees lipstick printed onto his vellum
painted with the patience of the monk

II

remove greenhouse plants
transform into frowns and laughs

hold the pen
write the letter
wipe the surface
blotted paper
everlasting ink

written in pencil, with a 'p'
wipe the surface.

his thoughts, soaked in the ink of everlastingness, blot the white paper.
large rivers separate punctuation.

—

Chinese ochre Rorschach
no lipstick.
only striped wallpaper
painted with patience

III

inspiration to write – on the spot – all (im)perfections

—
he wonders if the L could be first
tongue click
he tries the "O"
sharpen the pencil to numb the mind
Chinese ochre Rorschach
the writing is on the wall

IV

all ingredients lie in front
ochre separates long rivers
all the words swell out of proportion.

—

he sees dotted cows and striped wallpaper
he longs for the mortification of the flesh
Chinese ochre Rorschach
request to return to the cell

V

words ooze out of his mind
really small doses
watch her unfold the mirror
mirror over matter
perfect (dis)proportions
lipstick is printed onto vellum

—

request to return to his cell
Chinese ochre Rorschach
knitting distance into particles
the striped wallpaper absorbs him
addicted!

VI

Rusalka is wandering in the swamps
stop floating on the foggy clouds
light is divided into waves and particles becoming waves before reshaping
themselves again into particles

—

Chinese ochre Rorschach
a string of vowels
imprisoned in a box of consonants
only punctuation serves a key role

VII

the staircase seems like dripping with chocolate
his fingers are full of it

———

Chinese ochre Rorschach
striped wallpaper
dotted cows
a vellum of patience
all tastes surrender
to the hole in one

VIII

cacao powder is dwindled on rice pudding
golden spoons are requested
food = on the table
senses send signals
brain analyzes
see, smell, touch, taste
all this is in 0's and 1's
no 2's

—

Chinese ochre Rorschach
wallpaper stripped
cows dotted
vellum stretched
surrender
to the whole

IX

a wave of particles
words out of proportion
hold the paper
write the surface
blot the letter
wipe the pen
everlasting ink
his thoughts got stuck at the 'p' of 'poet'
the 'm' carved with a needle
cracks lost meaning
small rivers separate longing from downstream punctuation
sail through vowels

Chinese ochre Rorschach
wallpaper stripped
cows graze
vellum lipstick
surrender
to the one

Undercurrent

In the Future (a work in Progress) II

in the future
there will be
home
home to pot a plant
home to listen to music
home to paint the mirror
home to visit the web
home to applaud at eight
home to watch the news
home to chat with your loved ones
home to read
home to talk
home to walk
home to work
home to study
home to teach
home to live
home to think about
what to do in the future
when there will be
home
home to re-pot a plant
home to listen to your music
home to paint the other mirror
home to visit a webshop
home to applaud at eight
home to watch the news
home to chat with your loved ones
home to read
home to talk
home to walk
home to work
home to study
home to teach
home to live
home to think about

what to do in the future
when there will be
home

home to sop a plant
home to listen to more music
home to paint the mirror that fell on the floor
home to visit your webcasts
home to applaud at eight
home to watch the news
home to chat with your loved ones
home to read
home to talk
home to walk
home to work
home to study
home to teach
home to live
home to think about
what to do in the future
when there will be
home

What Is Life?

I gaze at the stars, drown particles
waves of unconsciousness in a mirage

a cat within, indecisive
thirsty

I am, cause I shine
I am, cause I radiate
I am, cause I bring
death & destruction
life starts at the ping of a microwave
gaze at the world
in a glass of water

a cat within, indecisive
thirsty

particles beam onto retina
Do you feel the light?
Do you radiate life?
Do you see breastfeeding as a political action?
Black Knight hits White Bishop
White Pawns lynch Black Knight
black hole sucks all
matter

a cat within, indecisive
thirsty

tea measured in leaves
cubes of salt, drilled not shaken
a glass, half empty
a bell fathoms distant recording
I do phone home
with the index
but no answer

clarity fades
particles drift

a cat within, indecisive
thirsty

in the beginning there was the word

but no ink
a parchment as light
different forms
waving goodbye

a cat hits a flask
stumbles over
nine lives

The Day After

Now *they* know where *everybody* lives

forget about tormenting storms
watch
raindrops pour down onto
raindrops falling freely onto
raindrops swelling into
swarms drenching into
puddles becoming
brooks broadening into
rivers running into
streams dissolving into
fluxing floods

                                        look at the lightning
                                        snapshot of reality

after the laughter they went away
they gathered words
only the letters matter
gathered and pasted
on papyrus scrolls

Where were You when we perished into oblivion?

Last Press Conference by Caligula After he Appointed Incitatus Vice-President Before Pushing the big red Button in his Penthouse on Live TV

Frankly, my dear, I don't give a damn!
You're gonna need a bigger boat.
May the Force be with you.
I've a feeling we're not in Kansas anymore.
I'm going to make him an offer he can't refuse.
You talkin' to me?
There's no place like home.
The first rule of Fight Club is you do not talk about Fight Club.
Here's looking at you, kid.
Why so serious?
Yippee Ki Yay, motherfucker.
We'll always have Paris.

The greatest trick the devil ever pulled was convincing the world he didn't exist.

After all, tomorrow is another day.

There can only be One

there can only be one
Head and Shoulders
of a failed state
'opening our borders'
he complimented the news anchor
'is what made us great again'
he manstruated perfect solutions
to complex dreams, Playmobil-phantasms, Lego-concoctions
saving his world in 140 characters
space included
by the tower invested in him
he nuked the ugly
he tartared the bad
he fired the good
"Yippee Ki Yay, motherfucker"
he shouted at his cleaning lady
as she changed his diapers.

Drone Talk Transcripts #2: The Uncensored Version

[snake72]   We are now tracking three vehicles going south

[orchid54]   Roger, ground force commander's intent is to destroy the vehicles and the personnel, right now lotus87 is showing that the individuals aggressing the vehicles are holding cylindrical objects in their hands »radio static«

static radio shatter

[snake72]   Roger, go back there, do you see a riffle

[orchid54]   affirmative, that IS a riffle

[snake72]   Roger orchid54, please advise, it is a riffle

[orchid54]   Roger that, you have the authority to wipe them bastards out

[snake72]   Roger orchid54, will do so with pleasure, lock on missile

static radio shatter

[lotus87]   dinner is served!

static radio shatter

[lotus87]   don't let it go cold! If it get's cold, I'll bin it. You won't get food

[snake72]   »radio static« mission completed, goin' back to base.

Epilogue

Cardinal Points

(4Kat   - and also 4Peter)

Four is the number of corners on a standard page
Four is the number of sides on a standard page
In the middle of these sides - halfway between the corners -
Cardinal Points are marked
To the north - a bearded redhead recites Beowulf with a castrate - there is
no sun
To the east - a rusalka analyzes Tambov poetry using Tartu semiotics - the
moon rises like blood
To the south - an elephant searches his Hannibal to cross pink alpine
peaks - the heat scorches the page
To the west - the water of the ocean deepens with every Kon-Tiki trying to
catch up with the Galician, the Painted and the Niña - the sea sets into the
broadening sky
Four is the number of triangles appearing when connecting the corners on
a standard page
Four is the number of rectangles appearing when connecting the cardinal
points on a standard page
Four is the number of ways a standard page can be folded in two
Three is the number of parts one folds a letter to fit into an "American
envelope"
Two is the number of editors to work on the book
One is the number of poets writing the book (without taking into account
the number of poets inspiring the poet writing the book)
Zero is the number of days until

I Am the Last Poet

I am the last poet, published {*insert image here*} before the wall

<play ominous music here>

the dingy I sailed in was recycled into art
sold to the highest bidder to cleanse a conscience
{*insert video here*} and so I speak to you, reader of this text

<music played by a military brass band here>

what have we done to make our country
great minds sink alike into the perspective of
<hip-hop or rap music here> me, myself and I
vegetating in front of 24/7 prepared infotainment

{fragments of political debates and news coverage here}

we wiki the world, sit on a terrace, watch the rain
slowly cleaning the window of the Agency of Covered-Up Truths
the world we have inherited: No Future (so belt that bomb)

Punk is death!   *<play punk music>*

The Future Is Bright, so cry me an ocean

<fairy tale music here> {*video of abundant green jungles*}

So do enjoy our own mass extinction event

Notes and Acknowledgments

A big shout out

to Boni Joi
   for editing and first reading the first
and last line of every book
to festival organizers
   for inviting me and sparkling the inspiration
for this book
to fellow poets
   for the long inspiring conversations
to my children
   unlimited source of inspiration
to my wife
   my infinite muse
to Belgian chocolate

Notes

Mare Nostrum — Brussels (Brussels Capital Region, Belgium), September 3, 2015. Written in pencil on used MIVB-STIB metro cards. Edited in Apple Notes, version 2.0 (284) and finalized in Microsoft Word for Mac, Version 14.1.0 (110310) in font style Courier New

Sid Meier's War on Terror — London, August 16, 2015. Written in Microsoft Word for Mac, Version 14.1.0 (110310) with font style American Typewriter

The Holy Trinity Bus Poem — Written during the flight from Durban to Brussels via Dubai after the Africa Poetry Festival 2018, inspired by a joyful conversation on the touring bus with the Holy Trinity — Vuyelwa Maluleke, Emmah Mabye and Nkateko Masinga, October 17-18, 2018. Written in Notes on iPhone 7. Edited in Microsoft Word for Mac version 16.35 (20030802) in font style American Typewriter

Conventional Stereotypes — November 5, 2017. Written in notes on iPhone 7 from Trivandrum airport to The Gateway Hotel Varkala (A Taj Hotel), the Kerala Backwaters, India. Edited in Microsoft Word for Mac version 16.35 (20030802), in font style American Typewriter

9/11 Memorial/One WTC — This poem was dedicated to Dianne T. Singer and Jennifer L. Howley and their unborn children. Written on a bench on the banks of the Hudson River, New York, USA on November 16, 2014, with a turquoise coloured pen in a Canson Universal Art Book (A5) on Canson Crob'art paper 96gsm. Edited in Apple Notes, version 2.0 (284), in Microsoft Word for Mac, Version 14.1.0 (110310). Finalized in Microsoft Word for Mac version 16.35 (20030802) in font style American Typewriter. Published in *The Poet Magazine*, Spring 2020, *War & Battle*

Molenbeek — Written on a bench on the banks of the brook Molenbeek, November 19th, 2015 at the Boudewijn Parc, Jette (Brussels Capital Region, Belgium). Written in Apple Notes for iPhone5. Edited in Microsoft Word for Mac, Version 14.1.0 (110310), in font style Cambria

In Honor of Hugo Pratt — Lyon, Musée des Confluences, exhibition: Hugo Pratt, lignes des horizons, July 28, 2018. Written in Notes version 4.5 (876.1) on iPhone 7. Edited in Microsoft Word for Mac version 16.35 (20030802) in font style American Typewriter.

Pictures of an Exhibition at Chhatrapati Shivaji Maharaja Vastu Sangrahalaya (Formerly Prince of Wales Museum of Western India), Mumbai — November 5, 2017. Written on notes on iPhone 7. Edited in Microsoft Word for Mac version 16.35 (20030802) in font style American Typewriter. Fragments in italic taken from the display panels at the textile exhibit at the Chhatrapati Shivaji Maharaja Vastu Sangrahalaya (formerly Prince of Wales Museum of Western India), Mumbai. (1) taken from a beaker text at the Chhatrapati Shivaji Maharaja Vastu Sangrahalaya (formerly Prince of Wales Museum of Western India), Mumbai.

Meaning — Magritte Museum Jette, Jette (Brussels), April, 29th, 2017. Written in Apple Notes for iPhone5. Edited in Microsoft Word for Mac version 16.35 (20030802) in font style Courier New.

Hunting Season — Tenerife, January 2nd, 2017. Written in Apple Notes for iPhone5. Edited in Microsoft Word for Mac version 16.35 (20030802), in font style Cambria

Magritte Tie with Eyes — Magritte Museum Jette, Jette (Brussels), April 29th, 2017. Written in Apple Notes for iPhone5. Edited in Microsoft Word for Mac version 16.35 (20030802) in font style Courier New.

The Habit of Speaking — Magritte Museum Jette, Jette (Brussels), April, 29th, 2017. Written in Apple Notes for iPhone5. Edited in Microsoft Word for Mac version 16.35 (20030802), in font style Courier New.

Ominous They Stand — November 4, 2017, Mumbai Harbor on the ferry to Elephant Island, India. Written on notes on iPhone 7. Edited in Microsoft Word for Mac version 16.35 (20030802), in font style Cambria.

Paradise by the Lakeside Light — November 6, 2017. Written in notes on iPhone 7 at the Fragrant Nature Lake Resort & Spa, the Kerala Backwaters, India. Edited in Microsoft Word for Mac version 16.35 (20030802), in font style Bookman Old Style

Mountain of Fat — November 7, 2017. Written in notes on iPhone 7, somewhere on the Southern backwaters between Monroe Island and Kollam. Edited in Microsoft Word for Mac version 16.35 (20030802) in font style Cambria.

It's Not the Stars Which Are Important — November 8, 2017. Written in notes on iPhone 7 somewhere on the Southern backwaters between Monroe Island and Kollam. Edited in Microsoft Word for Mac version 16.35 (20030802), in font style Cambria

What Defines Us Is How We Rise After We Have Fallen — November 11, 2017. Written in notes on iPhone 7 on the beach at Vakkom, India, Arabian Sea after conversations with Rati Saxena, Heike Fiedler, Koukis Christos, Bas Kwakman, Frank Keizer, Gökçenur Çelebioğlu, Hermant Divate and the festival volunteers of the 11th Kritya International Poetry festival. Edited in Microsoft Word for Mac version 16.35 (20030802), in font style Calibri

Past the Darkest Hour — On board of Aeromexico flight AM 26, Mexico April 18, 2018, 2:44 am. Written in Notes on iPhone 7. Edited in Microsoft Word for Mac version 16.35 (20030802), in font style American Typewriter

Maze Inc. — April 18, 2018, MEX airport till Eucalipto, CDMX, Mexico. Written in notes on iPhone 7. Edited in Microsoft Word for Mac version 16.35 (20030802), in font style American Typewriter.

Magic Dreams — CDMX, Mexico, April 19-22, 2018. Written in notes on iPhone 7. Edited in Microsoft Word for Mac version 16.35 (20030802), in font style American Typewriter.

Barcelona: I, II, III — May 11, 2018, Barcelona, Spain. Written in Notes on iPhone 7. Edited in Microsoft Word for Mac version 16.35 (20030802), in font style Baskerville.

Barcelona: IV, V — May 12, 2018, Barcelona, Spain. Created in Notes on iPhone 7. Edited in Microsoft Word for Mac version 16.35 (20030802) in font style Baskerville

Boy in a Box — CDMX, Mexico, April 21, 2018. Written in notes on iPhone 7. Edited in Microsoft Word for Mac version 16.35 (20030802), in font style American Typewriter.

Red River — Durban, Africa Poetry Festival 2018, inspired by a conversation with Matete Motsoaledi, room 1006, room Party, Belaire hotel, October 17-18, 2018. Written in Notes on iPhone 7. Edited in Microsoft Word for Mac version 16.35 (20030802) in font style American Typewriter

Of Ancient Books and Maps, the Quest and the Sea — Based upon "Tvoyage van Mher Joos van Ghistele, twelcke mach anders ghenaemt sijn: T'excellent, groot, zeldzaem, ende vreemt Voyage, ghedaen by wylent, Edelen ende weerden Heere, Mher Joos van Ghistele... Tracterende van veelderande wonderlijcke ende vreemde dinghen gheobserveert over d' Zee, inde landen van Sclavonien, Griecken, Turckyen, Candien, Rhodes ende Cypers." Written by Zeebout, Abrosius and (ed.) Joos van Ghistele and three Mercator maps of Cyprus. All part of the collection of the Bank of Cyprus Cultural Foundation. Commissioned by the 4th International Literary Festival, to the sea-girt shores of Cyprus, November 27 – December 1, 2019. Written in Notes on iPhone 7. Edited in Microsoft Word for Mac version 16.35 (20030802) in font style Calibri.

We Dance to It — Inspiration is a song by Matete Motsoaledi and "An orphan's cry, is music to our ears (we dance to it)"- Sepedi proverb. Written with the last mail of Pascal Verreth in mind. Thank you, inspirator and mentor. Thank you, Lucinda Sherlock for the line: "Remembering how we marked time together". Brussels, March 10, 2019. Written in Notes on iPhone 7. Edited in Microsoft Word for Mac version 16.35 (20030802) in font style Calibri.

Take This Body, Break It, and Forget I Ever Existed — inspired by talking to the poets taking part at the 4th International LIterary Festival, to the sea-girt shores of Cyprus, November 27 – December 1, 2019, edited in Word for Mac, version 16.34 on March 2. Written in Notes on iPhone 7. Edited in Microsoft Word for Mac version 16.35 (20030802) in font style Calibri.

No Nightingales in Nicosia — Inspired by the visit to Platres, Nicosia (both sides of the Green Line) and the discussions amongst the poets at the 4th International LIterary Festival, to the sea-girt shores of Cyprus, November 27 – December 1, 2019, edited in Word for Mac, version 16.34 on March 2, 2020, Font: Calibri, Font size: 12. Written in Notes on iPhone 7. Edited in Microsoft Word for Mac version 16.35 (20030802) in font style Calibri. Published in *The Poet Magazine*, Spring 2020, *War & Battle*

Modest & Free Interpretation of a Mussorgsky — reworked from the original version after a mail conversation with Lucie Blush

Cardinal Points — Paris, France, June 14, 2014. Written in Apple Notes for iPhone5. Edited in Microsoft Word for Mac, Version 14.1.0 (110310) in font style American Typewriter

I Am the Last Poet — This poem needs to be read out-loud in front of a huge crowd of cardboard portraits of the poet reading this poem

The reader needs to visualize this poem as printed in full color, with different font styles and font sizes to accentuate the meaning of it all.

The basic font style is in this poem Arial, the basic font size 12.

{*insert image here*}: font color = #F81F09.

<*play ominous music here*>: font color = #1992CF, font style: SNAP ICT; font size 20

{*insert video here*}: font color = #FC070A

<*music played by a military brass band here*>: font color = #AEB6BF, font style: Goudy Stout; font size 9,5

<*hip-hop or rap music here*>: font color = #D6EAF8, font style: Vladimir Script, font size: 36

{*fragments of political debates and news coverage here*}: font color = #E74C3C, font style: Algerian, font size: 9,5

<*play punk music*>: font color = #000000, font style: Old English Text MT, font size: 9,5

<*fairy tale music here*>: font color = #FCC7C9, font style: Edwardian Script ITC, font size: 9,5

{*video of abundant green jungles*}: font color = #ACA3A4, font style: Snap ITC, font size: 9,5

The last lines in this book are dedicated to H.E. Marc Mullie (10/30/1959 – 10/05/2020), Late Ambassador of Belgium to Australia, Cook Islands, Fiji, Kiribati, Nauru, New Zealand, Papua New Guinea, Solomon Islands, Samoa, Tonga, Tuvalu and Vanuatu; dear friend and valued critic. May these words accompany you o your voyages in the Dreamtime.

Long live anarchy.

Reviews

Deep blue sea on the canvas of poetry
when I turn the pages
of deep blue seas
I wave my sails
peacefully quilted
with parts of tales
never to be told.

In ancient Indian literature, blue is the color of purity, of peace and of deepness, that is why in ancient Indian theater, the deities had blue colored faces. But when a poet from European country speak about blue, I am sure he is not far away from these meanings. Poets around the world carry, similar kinds of emotions. In fact, the blue is the color of the poetry, which a poet should write, the poetry on which he sails and gets the stories of the unknown emotions and places which were unknown to him also. The blue is deepness, the vastness the eternity and sometimes the life after death.

In this most difficult times, when nature is getting destroyed, people are abandoned, mountains are treeless, and people are thrown out of their own land. The Blue is a need of time —

The blue is need of time. When a person /*the world is suffering from anorexia/expressionism of overflying cargo planes/treeless mountains bombarded with flower/of departing troops and abandoned refugees/left to the enemy's free hand*

The peace is an energy or awareness, which generates the fire of thoughts. In reality the peace is very powerful, which works deep in the hearts. The poet says– *I gave you fire to burn away the image, /water to deepen the distance/ by the tower invested in him/he nuked the ugly/*

The sea should be a sea in its corrector, vast, full of lives, deep, and which takes. In ancient literature,. the deities have the quality of a sea, deep, peaceful and life oriented. But when these qualities change the life of the Universe:

The sea should just be sea/the waves may not be confined to concrete jaws

But what do we do? We build walls, and that is how our souls remain closed:

you build a big wall and your soul is confined within the wall.

I love these lines of the poet the stars are not important, but importance is darkness, which is in our eyes. And that darkens made us give importance to stars as they help to get light.

It's not the stars which are important/it's the darkness in our eyesight/ what is the surrounding in which you thrive?

I remember the Upanishad takes from darkness to light, take us from death to life....

At the end, the poet expresses the need of vastness of blue of the universe- it is for free thinking, free emotions, free ideas, and we need a free life as a human, not for ourselves, but all living or nonliving things of the world.

Free thinking is a business
Free thinking is valuing the possible
Free thinking is possible
Free thinking is a feeling

At the end, I want to tell that I was bit astonished to read these insightful poems, as I know Philip as a very strong performer. Most of the time, while performing, we have to become a bit loud, and loose the contact with a deep quite inner world, these poems brings the inner world of the poet, and that is completeness of the poet.

These poems to be read by all of us, quietly, in the mind and feel in the soul

I congratulate the poet for such wonderful work

Rati Saxena

Philip Meersman knows that to be alive is to be on the move. The poems in *There Is Blue Somewhere* give off a restless, perceptive energy in which even sitting still involves exploring a constant surge and flow of information, physical, mental, psychological, often all at once. Both in content and inventively shifting structures, Meersman's poems show readers how many different ways experiences reach us and shape who we are.

Playful, hilarious, generous, sometimes sad or overwhelming, the lines in There Is Blue Somewhere are perfect companions for helping to realize that the way we go somewhere may be more important than wherever we think we're trying to get.

Mark Wallace, *Professor in the Literature department at California State University San Marcos*

There Is Blue Somewhere opens on an ocean teeming with humanity and its various waste products. This surreal vista that Philip Meersman paints is *Mare Nostrum*: a mirror image of the mess we have created. Over fat mountains, across a Mediterranean filled with hopeless life-rafts, and through drone-filled war-zones, crowds of beggars, and swarms of social media influencers, no human foible escapes Meersman's caustic, socially conscious gaze. This impassioned, witty, elegiac book captures the performative power of Meersman's work on the page, confronting us, demanding, *Where were You when we perished into oblivion?*. These are unflinching poems that defy the reader to ignore the message they carry: that we must change our lives.

Jessica Traynor, writer, *dramaturg and creative writing teacher based in Dublin*

I enter the world's navel
humble
I bow to the Tlatoani

So goes the journey of the 21st century Odysseus into the *Magic Dreams* of our civilization punctuated with *cannabis and excrements, concentrated urine, a public toilet.* It is at once a familiar and strange landscape... the world we live in right this moment but have never been articulated as it is. Philip Meersman takes our hands and guides us to step out from our mundane consciousness, fogged with logic, reasons, facts, history, and information, all in quotation marks. His ship is built with everyday language but equipped with the sails of quick improvisation and oars of exquisite word-play. And he has an ancient sextant to set his course, called love: love that goes beyond the humanity towards this planet and the cosmos around it. This is the endeavour that is rooted deep in the cultural heritage of Europe but free and solo in the vast ocean of our post-singularity future. There got to be *Blue Somewhere*.

Yasuhiro Yotsumoto, *poet*

Philip Meersman is blue. So is his newest book. But not blue like they've both got the blues (although that's part of it, too). Blue like the sky on a beautiful blue-sky day. Like the water of life, reflecting heaven. Blue like eternity. And this day, this eternity -- which is also a book -- is at the same time a travelogue that contains multitudes: the road to Oz, where *toads were more* attracted to storks/flies to frogs; Caligula's last press conference (wherein he quotes Scarlett O'Hara and Humphrey Bogart, among others); a bench in New York City on the banks of the Hudson River where the poet scribbles notes with a turquoise coloured pen in a Canson Universal Art Book (A5) on Canson Crob'art paper 96gsm. For eternity to be possible, there has to be the blue of heaven and the blue of the blues — an answer to the question, *Where were You when we perished into oblivion?* Yes, an answer to that might be impossible. But a poem is always possible. And that's what this beautiful poetry collection is about: possibility.

Sharon Mesmer, *multi-genre writer and creative writing prof / techno-marm at NYU and the New School.*

In my first reading of Philip Meersman's second poetry collection, *There is Blue Somewhere*, I am initially struck and momentarily immobilized by *The Holy Trinity Bus Poem* in the Cycle of Eternity section of the book. The poem intrigues me not only because of the use of lowercase for all words except those referring to deity and profanity, but because the refrain in each stanza is so familiar to me; it is an inside joke shared by a few poets from the Poetry Africa 2018 cohort, a memorable yet arguably unholy phrase stemming from a poetry workshop. The refrain, which we later abbreviated to "MFSS" in order to avoid stares from astonished onlookers, is a clear example of how Meersman weaves strangeness into the mundane. In *The Holy Trinity Bus Poem*, there is indeed blue somewhere — *burn blue in screens/submerged in tweets and likes* — and this continues a pattern I identify beginning with the first poem in the collection, *Book of Life*, which opens with the words *when I turn the pages/of deep blue seas.*

In my subsequent rereadings of the collection, this pattern of references to the colour blue serves not only to tether me to a sense of linearity but also prompts me to disentangle myself from it and allow the eccentricity of the poems to take hold. Yes, there is blue somewhere — if one is willing to look closely enough — but there is more, too, if one's head is not submerged in the clouds as the book's cover illustration so aptly portrays. However, even in this unlooking, there is blue too. Meersman's poems are as real as they are surreal, as rooted to the ground as they are ethereal. This collection is a quirky and unforgettable masterpiece.

Nkateko Masinga, *author of Psalm for Chrysanthemums*

the boat knows where to take you
there is blue somewhere

Sashti Abda Poorthi

Printed in Great Britain
by Amazon